Raising the Bar in Marriage

A 31-Day Devotional

Donna Barbier

ISBN 979-8-88540-643-7 (paperback)
ISBN 979-8-88616-221-9 (hardcover)
ISBN 979-8-88540-644-4 (digital)

Christian Faith Publishing
832 Park Avenue
Meadville, PA 16335
www.christianfaithpublishing.com

Printed in the United States of America

I dedicate this marriage devotional to my amazing husband, Carl. You have always listened without judgment, spoken without prejudice, helped me without entitlement, understood without pretension, and, most importantly, loved me without conditions. Thank you for always putting God first and teaching me what true love is.

Introduction

Do you know a couple who's been married for twenty years or more? Do you ever wonder how those couples make marriage work? How do they thrive when so many marriages struggle just to survive—if they make it at all? Most marriages these days are unique if they last three or more years. My husband, Carl, and I get asked often, "How do you both act as though you're still on your honeymoon?" The answer is simple really because we still are! Our marriage is successful because of "building blocks." We are very purposeful about our marriage and about one another. With so many distractions in life these days, our relationship with each other comes directly behind our individual relationships with God.

This kind of marriage isn't a casual acknowledgment of each other; we are two people who are committed to one another, and who choose to find something to do every day that will make a positive impact in our marriage. If you are purposeful each day about doing one thing that is good for your marriage, think how impactful your marriage would be by all of the intentional things you did to strengthen it.

Wouldn't you begin to see the goodness in your marriage? Wouldn't your thoughts toward your marriage be more positive than negative? As you walk through this devotional for the next thirty-one days, look for the daily "building block" that will help you and your spouse build and strengthen your marriage into one that lasts a lifetime.

Note

Each day will be followed with daily scripture reading. Any guesses as to what the main "building block" is in marriage? The Bible! Use your Bible to look up the daily scriptures as you study God's Word. This devotional is a tool, but God's Word is the key!
Ephesians 5:25
Genesis 2:24

Today's Building Block

Commit to build and strengthen your marriage as you incorporate the "building blocks" for the next thirty-one days.

Raising the Bar in Marriage

Day 1

Let's start with the million-dollar question, "What does marriage mean?" While there are tons of opinions and most likely fantastic answers to this question, I want to share with you what God laid on my heart to share with you. Marriage means being there for each other no matter what! One thing my husband, Carl, knows is that I am always here for him during the good stuff and the bad. I have no doubt he is for me as well. While I feel we are both strong individuals, a strong marriage rarely has two strong people at the same time. It requires a husband and wife taking turns being strong for each other in those moments when the other feels weak. Your spouse should never have to face any obstacle without your full partnership, encouragement, and support. You might not always be able to offer the perfect answer or the perfect solution, but simply by offering yourself and your support, you can create a perfect opportunity for growth in your relationship.

Galatians 6:2

Today's Building Block

Discuss with your spouse about being each other's support system.

Raising the Bar in Marriage

Day 2

When was the last time you prayed for your spouse? There are so many ways you can pray. If you need ideas for what to pray about, simply ask your spouse if there's anything he or she would appreciate you praying for. Your prayers can also come from just being a student of your spouse. Pray for them in their work, as a spouse, as a parent, or for something they are struggling with. I think you will be amazed at what happens. Praying for your spouse connects the two of you with God. It helps you come alongside your spouse.

When I am praying for Carl, I look at him differently. Praying for him draws me closer to him. It shows me that we are on the same team and are working together as we navigate life. The really cool thing is it puts us in a partnership with God. I promise you; God will show up when you invite His involvement in your marriage through prayer! Does that mean that God will answer your prayer for your spouse exactly the way you are praying? Maybe, but maybe not. What it does mean is that God will answer your prayer in a way that is perfect for you and your spouse. Try praying today and see what happens. There is absolutely nothing to lose and a lot to gain.

Colossians 4:2

John 16:24

Today's Building Block

Pray for your spouse.

Raising the Bar in Marriage

Day 3

Do you and your spouse have fun together? I mean, come on, every couple has "fun" at the beginning of their relationship while enjoying each other's company. If you didn't, I kind of doubt you would be married! However, life does get in the way of having fun. Other things slip in and become a priority to each of you! Having fun together is made less of a priority as careers, children, family, and other things fight for your time and attention. However, having fun together should be made a priority in your marriage! Couples *need* fun inserted into their life.

What did you do for fun when you were dating or in the early part of your marriage? What sounds fun to you to do as a couple today? It doesn't have to be an elaborate date or getaway. It could simply be a zoo date which happens to be Carl and I's personal favorite. Or a night of miniature golf. Or a day date where you take a walk on the river walk. What's important is setting aside time each week with no agenda other than time with each other and enjoying life together!

Block time out on your calendar for each other and do not sacrifice it! It can recharge and supercharge your marriage.

*Also…*laugh…*a lot!* When someone asks how we stay happy, Carl always says the key is to "make her smile and laugh daily!" That statement alone always makes my heart leap because Carl always finds ways to do just that!

Ecclesiastes 5:18–20

Today's Building Block

Decide on a "fun thing" to do together this week. Then do it!

Raising the Bar in Marriage

Day 4

Have you ever been around someone who is always complaining about their spouse? It's like their spouse never does anything right and even when they try, they get it wrong. Nothing good ever results from those negative words. They are laying a foundation of negativity in their marriage and their spouse gets slammed without even knowing it. It's a no-win situation.

One really good way to grow your marriage is to brag about your spouse to someone else. First, it is a great witness and example of a Christian marriage. Second, it keeps our thoughts about our spouse on the positive side. Another benefit of speaking positively about your spouse occurs when someone else tells your spouse what you said about them. Your husband or wife is a gift to you from God. Thank God for your gift *daily* and start talking about your spouse to others in a positive way.

I'm going to leave you with this thought: Nothing changes if nothing changes, and the change should start with *you*!

Proverbs 15:1
Proverbs 16:24
Proverbs 31:26

Today's Building Block

Brag on your spouse today.

Raising the Bar in Marriage

Day 5

A couple of days back, we talked about praying for your spouse. Today, I want to discuss praying as a couple. It's extremely important in a marriage to go together to the Father as one!

Carl and I are very careful to be purposeful and intentional in prayer. We come to God as *one*! We praise our Father, we thank Him for the abundant life He has given us. We thank Him for the blessings and favor He has shown and will continue to show us. We praise Him! We then make a point to be specific with our prayer. Our prayers are not wishes. They are spoken words where only the move of God can bring change! All the while, our hearts are to stay in God's will. When we are praying for direction for our lives, we wait for God to answer. We don't move without Him!

As humans, it's very easy to see life through our eyes and pray accordingly. God sees the big picture and answers accordingly. If we truly believe that God is good, which He is, then we need to believe that His answers to our prayers are perfect for us.

Do you and your spouse pray together? Are your prayers specific, and are you both willing to do your part when God answers?

Isaiah 55:8–9

Today's Building Block

Begin praying together! Be specific and intentional with your prayers then watch God bring change in your marriage!

Raising the Bar in Marriage

Day 6

How much time per day do you spend with your spouse? I read a survey that said most married couples spend five minutes or *less* together! Before marriage, those same couples spent at least three hours a day together! That is twenty-one *hours* a week *before* marriage and thirty-five *minutes* a week *after*. *Wow!*

When Carl and I were dating, we spent as much time possible with each other. When we were apart, we spent that time on the phone talking for *hours*. Then we got married and life changed. In the beginning, his job gave him a few weeks off to get married and get moved into our new home. When he had to go on his first job out of town, I cried my eyes out the night before he left. I couldn't bear the thought of him not being with me. Carl knew at that moment that I hold our time together as a precious commodity. To this day, we make time. We do not take it for granted, and we make the most of it. It's important to us, and it optimizes our marriage in so many ways. We refuse to drift apart! Another key,

Carl and I also know the closer we draw to God, the closer we get to one another! There's a connection that can only be experienced in His presence.

What about you and your spouse? Are you at five minutes, three hours, or somewhere in between? Is your relationship closer now than it was this time last year, or are you drifting apart? If your marriage is going to grow, there are no shortcuts to time spent together. Start being purposeful. If you are currently spending zero time together, begin spending at least five minutes a day with each other. Make it the most connected five minutes you can imagine—talk, touch, listen to one another.

You will be amazed at the difference it will make in your marriage. Do not stop there! Your time spent together needs to grow! It's vital for your marriage to thrive! The other vital key? God! He's the glue at the center of it all! You must keep Him there; drawing closer to Him brings you closer to one another!

Ecclesiastes 9:9

1 Peter 3:1–6

1 Peter 3:7

Today's Building Block

Spend five *purposeful* minutes connecting with your spouse, but do not stay there. Build from the five minutes as days go by until it grows into precious cherished time spent your marriage deserves.

Raising the Bar in Marriage

Day 7

Do you know that it's very important to praise your spouse daily? They need to know that you are their biggest cheerleader and that you are proud of them and their accomplishments!

When Carl puts effort into something, especially the efforts he makes for me, I do my best to tell him how much it means to me. It may be something as simple as fixing me a cup of coffee first thing in the morning. That simple act of love and the feeling of him taking care of me blesses my heart! I want him to know how appreciative I am of him—always! I want him to hear as much praise from me as he does from anyone else, *more* than anyone else! I tell him every day about how much I love him, and how amazing he is—because he is. I want him to *know* that I am his biggest fan! I *do not* want to leave that door open for others to tell him how awesome he is before hearing it from the one God chose for him. That's so important to me. As his wife, I'm his affirmation engine! I need him to lack for nothing from me in our marriage.

Do you praise your spouse? Do you praise them enough? Are they lacking from you? You have to remember, you are your spouse's gift from God, and you are created in His image! Are you reflecting that image?

If you haven't been looking up the scriptures I've been adding to each devotional, make sure to go read these! See what the Word says and *live it*!

Ephesians 4:29

Proverbs 25:11

Proverbs 12:25

Today's Building Block

Praise your spouse for one thing today, and I challenge you to do it daily.

Raising the Bar in Marriage

Day 8

Today's "Building Block" question to yourself is: "How have you been selfish in your marriage this past week?" Ugh! I hate that question because it always nails me. If there's even the slightest moment when I put myself before God and my husband, I twinge. It freaks me out! I wish it only affected me because that would be easier for me to take. But it doesn't just affect me. You see, when I move God out of first place and put myself first, I move Carl out of second place, and not only does that hurt my heart, but if I don't realize it and fix it, it will affect our marriage big time. Then guess what? It trickles down to other areas of my life. Life becomes just one big train wreck. If I allow it. When you insert love into a relationship, love is selfless! Because I love God and Carl more than myself, it helps me keep myself at bay. My life is not my own! My life is God's first and then at one with my husband. Removing yourself is hard when you're first working on it. Have I been selfish in my marriage this past week? I'm pretty sure I have at some point. Am I giving up? No. With God's help, I will remove my selfishness and put Him back in first and Carl back in second. It is the only way it works! I know by putting everything in God's hands, I can walk away from selfishness. So can you!

Philippians 2:3–4

James 3:16–17

Today's Building Block

Pray and seek God for answers! Ask Him to show you—*you*! Have you been selfish this week? If so, what do you need to do today to fix it? Think hard!

Raising the Bar in Marriage

Day 9

The following scripture is everything! "Husbands love your wives just as Christ also loved the church and gave Himself for her!" (Ephesians 5:25 NKJV).

In today's devotional, I am sharing with you a prayer that was written by my husband, Carl, while he was leaving for a job in Germany. Being states apart is one thing, but countries, that's another. It's these kinds of prayers for our marriage that provide strength. Have you ever heard that a three-cord strand isn't easily broken? Well, our marriage is five cord: Carl, me, the Father, the Son, and the Holy Spirit.

"While in Germany, I *pray…for my marriage*!

Father, when mankind was created, You provided a partner for him. Now, I have found Donna to be my life partner, my wife, my soul mate, to complete me in every area of my life.

I know that I have obtained favor from the Lord because Your Word says that a man who has found a wife has found a good thing and is highly favored by God! Thank

You, Father, for giving me Your Grace to receive what I do not even deserve!

I purpose in my heart to provide leadership to my wife, Donna, the way that Christ does to His Church, not by being dominant and or commanding, but by cherishing her in love.

Help me to give *all of me*, in love for her, exactly as Christ did for the Church! A love marked by giving of myself, not getting. Help me to always put her needs and desires above my own, just as You laid down Your life for us. We are the body of Christ, together, in one accord, and when I love my wife, I love myself. It is my desire to treat Donna the way she deserves to be treated and cared for because "she was Your daughter before she became my wife," and I will be held accountable to You on how I took care of Your daughter that You gave me as a gift.

Father, I honor Donna and delight and cherish her, not just accept her ungratefully, but I receive her with gratitude, overwhelmingly thankful and appreciative of her as a gift from You sent from heaven!

Father, help me as a husband to be gentle, compassionate, courteous, tenderhearted, and humble-minded. Let Donna and I live together with Your peace in our hearts, in our family, and in our home.

As we stand in unity, we are assured that our prayers are not hindered in any way and are effective to tear down strongholds and defeat anything that would come against us or our family!

Lord, we are aware that our marriage is growing stronger day by day because it is founded on Your Word, rooted and grounded in Your love, and have You as the central cornerstone that we are anchored to, to build our marriage and life upon.

Father, we thank You for the quality of marriage that Donna and I share, in Jesus' name. *Amen*!"

Ephesians 5:25–33

Today's Building Block

Make love and honor intentional in your marriage today!

Raising the Bar in Marriage

Day 10

Is your marriage filled with romance? Has the romance faded? It's a "cultural truth" that marital romance gradually dies over time. This becomes a self-fulfilling prophecy when we accept it as fact. We get married, the romance is great, but after a few years (usually when kids come into the picture), it begins to fade. We think the fading romance is the norm, so we accept it and move on. *No!* Don't accept it! Today I want to blow that "cultural truth" out of the water. Romance does not have to fade. In fact, I would say romance in your marriage should grow year after year! Maybe we should stop and define romance. It's not what your mind automatically goes to! Romance is not sex, okay! *But* sex can become romantic. Romance happens when a husband and wife are purposeful about finding ways to express their love for each other every day. It may be an act of kindness, doing something for your spouse you know they would love or enjoy; it may be the act of affirmation by leaving your spouse a love note on the bathroom mirror every once in a while; it may be an act of service like helping out around the house or simply filling their coffee cup. Find out what your spouse's love language is! There is a book out there that's fantastic! Romance can be sitting in church hearing God's Word with your husband's arm around you—I feel so close to Carl in these moments— or my favorite, making alone time for each other a priority. When we consistently do these things, the sex will take care of itself. So whether you have been married one year, five years, or fifty years, if the romance has died, it is time to get the shock paddles out and bring it back to life!

Song of Solomon 8:6–7

Today's Building Block

Write down two things you think are romantic, ask your spouse to do the same, share them with each other, and be purposeful with the romance in your marriage!

Raising the Bar in Marriage

Day 11

During the time Carl and I were dating, I posted a cartoon of Rapunzel from the Disney movie *Tangled* holding a cast iron skillet up to Flynn Rider with the title "Christian Dating," and the caption read, "You better not get in the way of me loving Jesus!" Not only did I marry a man who truly loves me unconditionally, but he also leads me towards Jesus in a way a husband is supposed to lead his bride! I am very blessed to have a husband who leads by example, so together our marriage can lead by example! Is your marriage one who points other marriages towards Jesus? Are you and your spouse leading by example to those around you? What if your marriage was a light to everyone you know? What if you and your spouse lived your marriage each and every day in a way that made other couples want their marriages to look like yours? What if, as a couple, you prayed, served, gave, put God as number one, and put each other as number two every day? Then, what if, the couples who admired you began to do the same thing? Other people would begin to notice those marriages and want to emulate those couples. We would have a "marriage light" spreading to other communities and places around the world, and we would finally see that light coming over the horizon back to us because it would have traveled around the world. What would our world be like then? Can you even begin to imagine what could happen?

Carl and I desire to be that light for others. Since day one our marriage has been an awesome testimony. It just takes one marriage at a time to begin to ignite the fire. But it takes that one marriage to be intentional about being the light!

Philippians 2:14–15

1 John 4:7

Today's Building Block

Can God use your marriage to illuminate the world? What if you and your spouse said yes to God today about becoming a "marriage light?" Let God step in and shine His light on your marriage so you can shine for others!

Raising the Bar in Marriage

Day 12

Today we are talking about the three-letter word: S-E-X! Do you make time for sex in your marriage? For some of you, the answer may be a resounding yes. Believe it or not, some would say no or "sometimes." Sex in marriage is a gift from God (see Song of Solomon). It is not the most important thing in marriage, but next to growing together in Christ, it needs to be as important as husband and wife, as everything else. It draws us close. It is intimacy at its best. It is unique because the two of you are unique.

Intimacy in marriage tends to get put on the back burner when life gets in the way. We get busy with kids, work, housework, volunteer work, events, and _______________ (you fill in the blank). When we neglect intimate time together, we miss out on this incredible blessing from God. I believe that sex in a Christian marriage is different. Every couple can have the physical, emotional, and mental parts of sex. But because the Holy Spirit dwells in every Christian, there is a spiritual dimension of intimacy that non-Christians cannot reach. It all goes to a whole new level. The best sex possible is in the context of a Christian marriage.

Proverbs 5:18–19

Song of Solomon 4:10

Song of Solomon 6:12

Today's Building Block

Talk together about being purposeful in your sex life. Then follow through!

Raising the Bar in Marriage

Day 13

How often do you praise your spouse? We may think a good thought about someone but never end up sharing it with them—not that we keep it to ourselves on purpose, we simply let the moment pass. The other day Carl was talking on the phone; I was so impressed with how he was handling what seemed to be a very difficult situation. Hearing him deal with his job shows me how extremely smart he is; it was one of the first things that I noticed about him when we were dating. I found it extremely attractive—just sayin'! I thought that when he finished that call, I would tell him how proud I was of him, but I completely forgot. I'm good at telling him how handsome he is and how much I love him, but when it comes to praising him for his character, words, or actions, I need to learn to say it when I think it and say it more often! When people tell me something positive, they witnessed about Carl, it makes me so proud to be his wife! I certainly need to remember to pass the words of others on to him as well! The point is that we need to verbally communicate those good things to our spouses. It is really good for both of us. It shows them that we care enough to say it, and it reminds us that our spouse is very special.

Proverbs 16:24

1 Thessalonians 5:11

Today's Building Block

Share something good about your spouse's character, words, or actions with them today!

Raising the Bar in Marriage

Day 14

Trust is a must! I cannot stress to you how important trust is in your marriage! When we have trust in a relationship, we often take it for granted. Then when we break trust with someone, we realize how hard it is to rebuild it. When trust is broken in one area of a marriage, it can bleed over into other areas. Say you lie about the money you've spent; you will probably lose your spouse's trust in financial matters. *But* what you don't realize is that one "little" lie causes your spouse to question everything you say or do, so you lose trust in other areas of your marriage as well. You might say, "I just told one lie. Why is that such a big deal?" Because it is! Trust is *huge*! Your peace in your marriage is broken without it! If you have trust in your marriage today, cherish it and guard it with your life. If trust has been broken, ask your spouse what you need to do to regain their trust—and then begin doing it. Start with forgiveness and build from there! Not having trust in your marriage is like allowing Satan to come in and mow right over it!

> Proverbs 11:3
> Proverbs 12:19
> Proverbs 12:22

Today's Building Block

Seek God's help in being trustworthy in every area of your life and marriage! If trust has been broken, ask for forgiveness *today*! Wasted time is time you will never get back!

Raising the Bar in Marriage

Day 15

What does "fighting for your marriage" mean to you? Maybe you've never really thought about it, or maybe you think it sounds like a lot of work! For me, fighting for my marriage starts with a solid foundation with three parts: Carl, me, and God. It is the three of us working together for an awesome marriage. The three of us can stand together against anything that would come against our marriage. Together we fight a culture that does more harm than good, especially to marriages. We build and strengthen our marriage through actions and activities that connect us, such as praying together, worshiping together, reading the Bible together, having date nights, spending quality time together each day, and making time for intimacy.

I look at it this way: if we do not purposefully fight for our marriage, we run the risk of settling for a marriage that is far from God's incredible design. That's not how I want my marriage! I want it to smack dab in the middle of God's plan for us!

If you are not fighting for your marriage, commit to start today! I encourage you to watch the movie *War Room*. Watch it together, watch it separately! Even if you've seen it, watch it again and take notes!

Matthew 9:6

Today's Building Block

Choose to fight for your marriage every day! Sit down together and make a list of things you *will* implement in your marriage to secure its solid foundation!

Raising the Bar in Marriage

Day 16

Do you see your spouse as a gift from God? When Carl and I look back over our story together, it is easy to see God's hand move in our relationship. It was not on either of our radars until the last minute that God placed us in each other's lives. Our story still amazes me and also helps me see that Carl really is truly a gift from God! He knew the husband I needed and the wife Carl needed.

The longer we are together, the more we see God's plan unfold. As a matter of fact, we are smack in the middle of a new season God is unfolding in our lives this very moment! It's exciting to know that we both want God's will!

We know our marriage has God's fingerprints all over it! I am sure there have been times when I've taken Carl for granted, but I always come back to the truth that God designed a gift that has been perfect for me, and that gift is Carl Barbier!

What about you and your spouse? Can you backtrack and see how God brought the two of you together? Can you see how perfect you are for each other when you embrace your differences? Can you see your spouse as a gift from God?

Proverbs 19:14

Proverbs 19:21

Proverbs 31:10

Today's Building Block

Thank God for the gift of your spouse today, then tell them! Let your spouse know they are a gift from God to you!

Raising the Bar in Marriage

Day 17

Have you ever wondered why the hardest people to forgive are sometimes the ones we love the most? Maybe it's because we let our guard down with them and become the most vulnerable. Maybe it's because we don't want to give them a chance to hurt us again. Even though we know that the possibility of reconciliation will never happen without forgiveness (which is usually what we truly desire), we hold on to our unforgiveness. Unforgiveness can be the root cause of a lot of what's wrong in your personal life, such as illness.

So what about your marriage? Is there something you are holding on to that is limiting your marriage? Is it keeping you from embracing all God has for your marriage? If there is, maybe today is the day to forgive. If you're not currently withholding forgiveness from your spouse, focus on keeping a heart of forgiveness for your spouse. It really goes back to God asking us to forgive—He has forgiven more than any of us can ever imagine. He is our model of what forgiveness looks like!

    Colossians 3:12–13

    Psalms 83:5

    Matthew 18:21–22

Today's Building Block

If you are harboring unforgiveness toward your spouse, begin the process of forgiveness today! Your life and your marriage depend on it.

Raising the Bar in Marriage

Day 18

What happens when a couple worships together? For Carl and me, worshiping together can actually happen anywhere as long as we are together, and our focus is on God. For today, let's narrow the focus to attending church together.

Do we automatically start worshiping when we walk into the service and sit down? Not at all. Our day begins serving three hours before; however, we do begin our day in prayer, and we are praying the entire time we are preparing for service. Once service gets started and the music begins, we let go of our minds, so we can enter into the presence of God, and we begin to worship Him—together! As we sing the same songs, hear the same message, and pray, we are connecting together with God. In these moments, I feel closer to God and closer to Carl.

Carl and I have been worshiping together since before we were married, but the experience is always transformative—every single time. This really came into focus for me the first time Carl had to be out of town for work, and I had to attend church alone. I experienced the difference. Sure, I still felt God's presence, but I missed experiencing it with my husband. I can't really explain it in words, but I know it is part of that whole "two become one" thing that happens when you are married. I am so grateful to our God who came up with the idea of marriage in the first place! Here's the thing, our spiritual life together makes our physical life together just that much more amazing! Without giving God those moments together, our marriage probably would not be the amazing marriage it is! It's God working through each of us individually and He alone that makes our marriage one for the books!

Colossians 3:16
Hebrews 12:28–29
1 Chronicles 16:29
Revelation 4:8

Today's Building Block

First things first, *commit* to attending church together! Second, as you attend church, go with the anticipation of encountering God and worshiping with your spouse! It truly is transformative!

Raising the Bar in Marriage

Day 19

Protecting your spouse is *huge*! This isn't just about physical protection, although that's part of it, it's also about protecting your marriage. So many things are fighting for our time, attention, and hearts that it's wise for us to go into protection mode.

Conflict is inevitable, yet conflict helps us grow deeper in our marriage because we've learned how to navigate that relational hurdle. How well couples repair the damage from their conflict is a vital component to a long and successful marriage. Don't try to push an issue aside and avoid challenging situations. As you experience conflict, choose to fight *for* your spouse, *not* against them. Your spouse may feel hurt during the conflict, but don't intend to do that. Walk through conflict in a healthy way in order to protect your marriage! There should be a culture of honesty. Often, we don't want to be completely honest for fear that we'll be rejected by our spouse. It also could be that we don't want to hurt our spouse with the truth. We think that avoiding the truth will prevent pain, but in the end, it only causes more. Being honest with your spouse protects your marriage from deception. If we're honest in the little things, that will lead us to being honest in all things. Each spouse has their own load to carry, burdens to bear, and hardships to endure. Seeking to be empathetic in order to see the responsibilities your spouse has will help you learn how to serve them. When you do this, you'll be a step ahead, and they won't have to even ask. I do this with Carl all the time. I know his load is heavy. I look for things to help him lighten up! I try to stay a step ahead so that when he "gets there" he sees it's already done! Look for ways you can protect your spouse's schedule from being overwhelmed. Surprise them by doing a chore they normally do and do it for them. Incorporating these small things into your marriage will show your spouse that you truly care and desire to protect them.

Galatians 6:2

Ephesians 4:31–32

1 John 3:18

Today's Building Block

In what area do you need to improve in your marriage? Growing through conflict, honesty, or being a step ahead? All of them? Ask God and seek your own heart, then discuss it all with your spouse!

Raising the Bar in Marriage

Day 20

Harvard Law School lists about two hundred action words that students can use to describe their experiences and accomplishments. There are words like *adjusted, balanced, counseled, illustrated,* and *served.* Guess what word is not in this extensive list? *Love.*

The dictionary lists three different uses of the word love as a noun. But when I use the word love relating to marriage, I use it as an action word. Love is how I express my affection for Carl by the way I do life with him. I want to serve him, cherish him, and have fun with him. Those desires may originate in my heart, but the way he sees them is through my actions—the things I do for him, the way I treat him, the activities that we do and enjoy together. I can tell him a thousand times a day that I love him, and he loves that, but what turns his head are the actions that are born out of my love for him.

What about you? What is an action of love you want to do for your spouse?

 Mark 10:45

 1 John 3:18

Today's Building Block

Today, turn your love for your spouse into one action of love! Then for the rest of the week, find a different action each day to share your love for your spouse.

Raising the Bar in Marriage

Day 21

God is first, your spouse is second, and everything else flows from that.

Life has many pieces and parts, and it can be difficult to put all the pieces together. Putting God first is a must. He created you and designed you perfectly, but the greatest truth is that apart from Him, we can do nothing. Putting your spouse second is vital! Your marriage depends on it. Your spouse is who you have vowed to love and cherish amongst other things! How serious do you take your vows? Occasionally, our priority list must be reordered for our benefit and the benefit of those around us. Our priorities are defined by how we spend our time. Time is a valuable asset and a resource that can be well invested or squandered if we aren't careful.

Take a few minutes and evaluate your schedule. What you make time for will answer the question of "what is your priority?" Is it God and your spouse? As you take a few minutes to evaluate, you can also brainstorm a few ways to shift things to keep the first things first.

1. Time with God in the Word and in prayer.
2. Time with your spouse in conversation and connecting. Re-read your vows! Are you doing the things?
3. Time with the people in your life that matter most!
4. Time reflecting on what you are grateful for what God has already done and being thankful for what He will be doing in your marriage and in your life!

John 15:5
Hebrews 10:24

Today's Building Block

Take a look at your schedule and block out time to connect with God and time to connect with your spouse. Evaluate the list of items above I gave you and set them for yourself.

Raising the Bar in Marriage

Day 22

Marriage was designed from the beginning of time to create a helper suitable for Adam so they could cultivate and work the garden together. God declared that it wasn't good for man to be alone, and His solution to the problem was Eve. She was not the problem; she was God's creative solution and provision for man. God designed marriage and destined for us to have a good marriage. The day in and day out life may look and feel messy, but the truth remains—we said "I do" to the spouse we married "until death do we part." In the same way, what we believe about our spouse shapes how we act; what we believe about our marriage shapes how we act.

No matter what they may have said or done, your spouse is God's workmanship created in Christ Jesus to do good works that God prepared in advance for them to do—just like you. The same scriptures that apply to your life and speak to your true identity in Christ define the identity and life of your spouse as well. At times, we can allow the pride of "greater than" to rise up and call something bad that God declares good. Our spouse needs us to believe that they are good—uniquely designed, favored, and loved. In a world where situations, circumstances, people, and the enemy are trying to tell them who they are—or aren't, your greatest privilege is to tell them who they *are in Christ*! If they aren't acting like who they were created to be, call them out! Tell them they are a great man of God or an incredible woman of God. As they begin to believe it, their actions will start to line up with their belief. Right believing causes our behavior to change! But the change starts with the *one* person who speaks into their life the most—*you*! If you can choose to say, "Your marriage is good," "You're in it to win it," and "You're better together," then you will have a fighting chance against any and everything that comes against you.

Genesis 1:31

Ephesians 2:10

Today's Building Block

Declare that God is good, you are good, your spouse is good, and your marriage is good—daily! Make sure to relay it to your spouse! They need you speaking the right things into their life, into your marriage!

Raising the Bar in Marriage

Day 23

Who watches the reality show *Nailed It*? Some days I really think I nail it as a wife. I can almost hear the hostess from the show say those words. (Just a pun, not really!) But some days, it does seem to come easy. I'm in a good mood. I am patient. I express my love. I serve. I do all the right things and none of the wrong. I wish I could say I'm consistent in perfecting my role as wife every day, but I'm not. In fact, the days I nail it I feel are few and really far between. Now if you ask Carl, he probably would have a different answer than me as his wife. I am my own worst critic. He seems to block out all of my flaws. I feel it's because God covers them for me because I abide in Him! Thank the Lord He reigns over my personal life and marriage! I would be lost without Him, totally! As a wife though, most days I succeed in one or two areas. It's not that I don't want a home run every day, because I do, but my humanity gets in the way. So on most days, I can beat myself up for striking out, but God is teaching me to focus on the hits, not the misses. In other words, I may only do one thing right as a wife some days, but that one thing can make a huge impact or difference in my marriage—especially if it is praying with my husband or serving him or setting aside time to be with him. When I focus on the misses, I stay in a pile of regret. When I focus on the hit, I get excited and motivated to get another hit the following day. However, I do know that there are some things I can "polish up" on! Marriage is a journey. None of us will be the perfect spouse every day, but we can do that one thing that makes that huge impact or difference.

Colossians 3:16
1 John 3:24 (My personal "birthday" scripture)
Hebrews 12:28–29

Today's Building Block

Make a list of what you feel you do right and the things you feel you do wrong for your marriage! Discuss the list with your spouse. The discussion can lead you to "polishing up" in areas if you allow it. Carl and I call these times "our check-in moments." It helps to keep things in the light and not in darkness. Just try it!

Raising the Bar in Marriage

Day 24

When Carl and I married, we said from the beginning, "We *must* make at least fifty years together!" That would put me ninety and him ninety-four. It's our heart's desire to have a fiftieth wedding anniversary before God calls us home! God can do it for sure! So say your marriage makes it fifty years, and on that fiftieth anniversary, as family and friends gather to celebrate with you, someone asks, "What is your secret to a lifelong marriage?" how would you answer?

If someone had asked me that question in my early twenties, I think my answer would have been "love." I feel most young people would say that love was the key! When you're young, you're seeing the world through rose-colored glasses. Today, at the age of forty-six and having lived through experiences, I would answer that question quite differently. Sure, love is important, but love alone will not get you to the finish line. Carl and I know this for fact! My answer today would be commitment! Commitment to each other and commitment to God; a deep, etched-in-stone commitment that covers the good days, the bad days, and all the days in between. A commitment that never wavers, no matter what. That is the secret to going the distance.

Ecclesiastes 4:9–10

Proverbs 3:3–4

Today's Building Block

Renew your commitment to your spouse and to God!

Raising the Bar in Marriage

Day 25

When you love your spouse, it must go way beyond feeling the emotions that make you smile and feel tingly inside. The love God showed toward us is our guide in showing love towards others, especially towards our spouse! Loving Carl daily includes actively putting his needs above mine and honoring him—even when I don't feel like it. I get it, some days it's easier to love your spouse, and some days it's a choice. But you do make up 50 percent of your marriage! Think about that for a second! Prioritizing your spouse as number 1 above all others on this earth makes a huge impact! In the world we live in, we say yes to things that we probably shouldn't. I know Carl and I are both guilty of it because we are both givers and servers of others. But here's the thing, when you say yes to things you probably shouldn't, it's typically your spouse who gets pushed to the back of the priority line. We assume they'll understand, and they might, but consistently doing this will cause a ripple that'll be hard to overcome. So *choose* your spouse over every other earthly relationship. Prioritize your time with them so they'll feel valued, cherished, and loved. Take some time to ask your spouse this question: Do you feel like you're my priority? (This is part of mine and Carl's "check-in moments" I spoke about earlier in the week!) Then listen without defenses raised and be willing to make some changes. (Another huge key!) Now let's talk about showing affection towards our spouse. The word *affection* means "a strong fondness," which can be displayed in a variety of ways. We aren't all created equal when it comes to our needs, so it's wise to learn how your spouse receives and feels loved by you. It could be words, it could be physical touch or both. Maybe your spouse feels how fond you are of them when you do something for them because it shows they were on your mind. I am pretty sure Carl and I are all three! Have a conversation with your spouse about what makes them feel that you are displaying affection toward them and then make a daily plan to do just that. If you already know, what are you waiting for? You are 50 percent, remember?

1 Corinthians 13:4–7

Today's Building Block

Again, "check in" with your spouse! Include the questions I mentioned in the post! I'm telling you, being present with your spouse and sharing the deep things with each other will change your marriage for the better! In what area do *you* need to improve as your spouse's spouse? Prioritizing your spouse as number 1 above others, displaying affection, or both?

Raising the Bar in Marriage

Day 26

Words carry a lot of weight. When we speak to others, we can delight or depress, compliment or condemn, help or harm. The words that leave our mouths typically do one of two things: build up or tear down. When voices everywhere chip away at your spouse's heart, you get to be the one who speaks love, joy, hope, and peace into their lives. It's extremely important to me to always lift Carl up, not only to his face, which is the most important, but to others as well! Never tearing him down! And him the same for me.

Ask the Holy Spirit to be your internal alarm when words leave your lips that don't build up your spouse. You'll be amazed at the person they become simply because you adjust how you speak. As you go through each day, consider the words you speak to, over, and about your spouse. Choose to be your spouse's biggest encourager, not their biggest critic. Choose to be the person who wipes away their tears, not the one who causes them. Choose to become a cheerleader for your spouse's strengths instead of always pointing out their weaknesses. Encouragement is a simple but powerful tool to bring fuel to your marriage and joy to your spouse. Let your words bring life to them, not death!

Proverbs 12:25

Ephesians 4:29

Colossians 4:6

1 Thessalonians 5:11

Today's Building Block

Speak life into your spouse and watch how your marriage grows!

Raising the Bar in Marriage

Day 27

How well do you know your spouse? The Bible says that God knew us before we were formed in our mother's womb. While I know I do not know Carl on that level, I strive to know him. I want to know him so well that I know the move he's about to make and what he's thinking before he does. Just ask him! He will tell you. Why? Because I know that knowing him on a higher level brings our marriage to a higher level.

When you and your spouse first started dating, I'm sure it took no effort to think about them. It took no effort for you to want to learn more about them and wanting to know them on a deeper level. But, as time passes, especially into marriage, sometimes it doesn't come as easy as you might think. What does that mean? It means you have to make an effort to know them more. You have to pay attention to your spouse! If you're face-planted in your phone nonstop and having one-sided conversations, that's not enough atten-tion! It might not be daily, but often I learn something more about Carl. I know him well. He says I know him better than he knows himself. But do you know what knowing him on that level does? It makes him feel loved, appreciated, wanted, cherished, and respected! Even little things like knowing he loves to get a text from me while he's off working during the day. Just saying "I love and miss you" shows him I'm thinking of him! It may not feel as romantic as face-to-face conversation, but the alternative is to neglect him, and if I love him, there's no way that will happen! Are you loving your spouse so much you want to know them more? It doesn't matter how many years you've been married. I guarantee if you took the time to pay attention, you will learn something new!

Jeremiah 1:5

Psalm 139:1

Today's Building Block

Make an effort today to learn something new about your spouse. Be intentionally attentive and present in your marriage!

Raising the Bar in Marriage

Day 28

Everyone has dreams and desires—I know I do, but so does Carl. So does your spouse, the same as you! Sometimes we focus so much on our own dreams and desires for our personal lives that we forget that the one God gave us to journey through life with has dreams and desires of their own. Carl and I have come through so much in our life before God inserted us in each other's lives. Our dreams and desires have changed at the ages of forty-six and fifty than what they were when we were in our twenties. Our main desire is to focus more on God, and what He wants for us than what we have ever dreamed for ourselves. I don't even want what I wanted for my life when I was twenty. And let me tell you, being in the will of God as a married couple out-desires, out-dreams your own desires and dreams! Especially when you ask God to guide you together and your life moves in the same direction. There's nothing else like it! But I understand that you and your spouse both have ambitions—careers, talents, hobbies. Some dreams appear attainable and within reach, while others might seem monumental and beyond your abilities. As mentioned before, this world can be ugly, and people can say and do things to squash your dreams. Spend some time asking your spouse what their dreams and desires are—truly listen to them. Then together, spend time in prayer asking God for direction. This is where God will hold up the center of your marriage. If He gives you both the green light, encourage your spouse to step out of their comfort zone. Let them know you're willing to help. Sometimes their dreams will inconvenience you, which is an amazing opportunity to show them you support them and are willing to walk with them to achieve those dreams. To truly be one in this life, letting God guide you both in the direction your lives should go—together—is a major key to having a happy marriage.

1 Thessalonians 5:11

1 Corinthians 13:4–7 (I use the love chapter a lot)

Today's Building Block

Ask, seek, and move! Ask your spouse about their dreams and desires, seek God for the direction together, and then together, begin moving in the direction God has set before you!

Raising the Bar in Marriage

Day 29

*T*he *social media trap*: this is a *biggy* for both Carl and me. Honesty and transparency are vital in a marriage and that goes for what goes out into the world. The world is basically being run on social media; however, we also know how toxic it can be for your marriage! Guard your marriage! And yes, it matters how rooted you and your spouse are in God as to whether your marriage can withstand the social media age. So here we go.

Don'ts

1. Don't have a secret account. There's no place for secrets in a marriage.
2. Don't hide your password. If you've got nothing to hide, giving your spouse unrestricted access to your email and social media accounts should not be an issue. Carl can pick my phone up anytime and look at any app, message, or email.

3. Don't block your spouse from your posts. Accountability is huge. If your spouse isn't on your social media account as a "friend," you already have a problem!

4. Don't use social media as your relationship fixer. Want to know what to do about an issue in your marriage? Seek Christian counsel. Someone rooted in the Word.

5. *Biggie.* Don't play with a flame from the past! (Or create new ones!) Messaging, commenting, liking, or reaching out to an old flame—or anyone of the opposite sex—is only going to get you burnt. Do not be tempted by predators looking to destroy what God put together! *This is where you use the block button!*

Do's

1. Do ask before posting! Before you post a personal issue, ask your spouse if they mind, and if they do, respect their wishes, and leave it off of social media.

2. Do stay positive. Lifting your spouse up on social media is a good thing! Do it often!

3. Do post pictures of you and your love. Facebook is meant to show the world the best parts of your life and your spouse should be just that.

4. Do take breaks. Social media has a way of consuming our thoughts, so much so that we are more

focused on Facebook than truly enjoying our time with our spouse. Focus on them when they are in front of you instead of how many "likes" you are getting on your most recent post. There's nothing like having the undivided attention of your love when you're in the midst of a conversation.

5. Do tag your spouse in your posts. I attach Carl to pretty much everything I post. It keeps me accountable to him on the things I am posting!

6. It's a great thing to set your profile with both you and your spouse! Also, go ahead and make your marriage "Facebook official" and tell the world who you're married to. Link those accounts!

7. The bottom line: social media is not good or bad. It's simply a tool that people use to communicate. However, when it is misused, it can cause serious damage to a marriage and have real consequences.

Ephesians 5:15–17

Today's Building Block

Check yourself and your social media. Have a real conversation with your spouse about how it is affecting your marriage.

Raising the Bar in Marriage

Day 30

Have you ever had a hard day, week, month, or season in your marriage? You're not alone.

I like to refer to our hard stuff in marriage as a "hard minute." The conversation in my head usually goes something like this, "We are having a hard minute Lord, we need you. Help us to see clearly, keep our hearts in alignment with your truth, our emotions in check, and let our words be few." Every single one of these pleas can be found in the Word of God and are there for our provision, protection, and direction. They guide us, realign us, and call us to more. Your "hard minute" and our "hard minute" probably look completely different, but that doesn't make them any less awkward or painful at the moment. We are fed the lie that marriage is bliss, and everyone else's marriage is perfect. They never fight, disagree, argue, or struggle. Well, let me be the first to tell you "they" very much struggle, argue, disagree, and fight.

A few months ago, Carl and I were frustrated with each other. I don't even remember what over, but I do remember we needed more communication. He was busy on the phone with work and church, and I was busy with some of the same. So conversations were one-sided, so to speak. But we stopped, recognized what was happening, and took a minute to direct our focus on each other and dealt with the situation immediately. The Bible says those who are slow to anger have greater understanding! We strive to have better understanding within our marriage. One thing we know, the enemy doesn't want us to be victorious, so he attacks to divide. Our marriage is strong and built on the foundations of God, but we must stay rooted in Him individually and together to withstand the attacks thrown our way. It starts with our connection with God. He doesn't move, He is unchanging, but life's circumstances can cause us to fall away before we even realize how far off course we might be. God's Word addresses every problem we face. Grab a truth from the Word of God about your current struggle or situation and use that scripture as your prayer to God.

Philippians 4:19
Ephesians 3:20
Hebrews 13:5

Today's Building Block

Be slow to anger and ask God to give you greater understanding.

Raising the Bar in Marriage

Day 31

There are several traits that will damage a marriage. Insecurities and indifferences in a marriage are big ones! Insecurity is always about you and is always fueled by fear, pride, unbelief, trauma, or rejection. It could be a combination of a few of them or all of them wrapped into one nasty little package. Perfect love casts out fear. The only perfect love is the love of God. If I expect Carl to take God's place and give me perfect love, then I am left empty and unhappy, and I would probably not realize why. By doing that, it would lead me to blame my husband for the void I have in my life when he's doing everything a husband should. I would allow my feelings and my needs to become my primary focus instead of acknowledging my husband and his love for me, and I would miss the God *in* him. Insecurity allows my feelings to drive the ship instead of allowing God's truth to guide us. If you allow insecurities in your marriage, it becomes a crippling weight robbing you of love, intimacy, and fun with your spouse. Do not let it!

Indifference comes into play when you quit caring. Somewhere along the way you stopped looking at your spouse, stopped trying to make things better; you both quit growing together and you put your marriage on the back burner. Indifference is a slippery slope and causes you to drift further and further apart. Without a real relationship with God, connecting conversations with your spouse, intimate encounters that are special and reserved just for the two of you, you begin going through the motions and believe that you can fall out of love. This is a lie of the enemy! Love is a choice, on display every day through your words and actions. Living to the fullest in marriage with Carl means: "Carl, I will look *at* you, I will look *for* you, and I will always look *out* for you. I'm *all in* and I'm *in it to win it!*"

    1 John 4:18

    Hebrews 12:2

    Ephesians 5:21–33

Today's Building Block

Read today's scriptures together. Really take them all in. Discuss them and dig deep into your marriage. Choose to love one another through Christ who dwells inside each of you!

Lagniappe
Raising the Bar in Marriage

Day 32

One of our biggest marriage "no-nos" is going to bed angry or with hurt feelings. Carl and I do not fight or argue at all—we made a promise to one another that we are past those days in life! Life is too short to be angry, especially with the one God gave us to share our life with! We simply do not do drama! However, on those rare and challenging occasions when frustrations run high, avoiding each other is simply not the answer but may feel like the easiest thing to do at the moment. How do we deal? When we got married, we vowed we would not let the sun go down on whatever issues we had that day. Most of our past frustrations stemmed from comments that caused unintentional hurt feelings, and we are not okay with each other hurting! We deal with the issue by talking it out calmly and with love!

If your feelings are hurt, bury the urge to be offended. Talk about it with each other using a tone that projects love, not anger! Think about this, if your spouse is unaware of your feelings, how can they make it right? Bottling up and allowing frustrations to boil until your lid pops off is simply wrong, and it robs your spouse of the chance to fix the problem! By not exposing the problem at the moment, you're contributing negativity into the situation instead of helping you and your spouse deal with it and move on! If you bottle it up and sit it on the shelf to save as ammunition to fire later, then you are a problem in your dying marriage! You need to check yourself first before pointing blame at your spouse for all of the things that are wrong! It takes two to make a marriage and two humble spouses to make a good one!

Carl and I also have a "no couch" rule. There is no room for division in our marriage! We will not allow it! We did not get married to fight or spend time apart. We simply have no space for hurt, anger, bitterness, or resentment to set up camp and grow in our marriage. We encourage you and your spouse to do the same! Axe it out of your marriage before you allow those things to kill it!

Ephesians 4:26

Today's Building Block

Do not keep things hidden from your spouse; especially if you're offended or hurt! Talk to each other, clean the slate, and vow to never allow the sun to go down on your anger.

Lagniappe
Raising the Bar in Marriage

Day 33

I doubt any of us would deny God's role as the "Potter" of our lives, but how are you doing at being the "clay"? Are you allowing God to mold you into who He created you to be, or are you fighting to stay in control?

Think about your marriage. How different would your marriage look like if you were allowing God to mold you into the husband or wife you should be? The change that needs to take place in your marriage starts with *you*! That change begins with you surrendering to God like the clay in the potter's hands! Examine your life and ask yourself, "How *moldable* am I by our great God?"

If you feel God is not using you, if you feel like your marriage isn't what it should be, if you feel like giving up, then you need to check yourself and realize that you're not allowing God be the God of your life!

Here's a statement you need to ponder: Our moldability determines our usability!

Jeremiah 18:2–6

Philippians 2:13

Isaiah 45:9

Today's Building Block

Sit down with God and do a "self-check." How moldable are you? Really examine your marriage and ask God to take over as the Potter to your clay and mold you into the husband or wife He wants you to be!

The End

About the Author

Donna Barbier is a South Louisiana native with over twenty years of experience in ministry. Her passion, along with her husband, Carl, is to help couples know who they are in Christ as individuals so together they can live the marriage God designed for them. Her prayer is that this devotional reaches those who need it the most.

www.ingramcontent.com/pod-product-compliance
Lightning Source LLC
Chambersburg PA
CBHW051259160726
47994CB00003B/1236